GARDENING
WITH
GOOD BUGS

GARDENING
WITH
GOOD BUGS

Erin W. Hodgson, PhD

SILVERLEAF
PRESS

To my 3-year old niece, Chloe, who is able to
identify more insects than most adults can.

Silverleaf Press Books are available exclusively
in the United States and Canada
through Independent Publishers Group.

For details write or telephone
Independent Publishers Group, 814 North Franklin St.
Chicago, IL 60610, (312) 337-0747

Silverleaf Press
8160 South Highland Drive
Sandy, Utah 84093

ISBN-13: 978-1-934393-01-7

CONTENTS

PREFACE

Thank you for your interest in this book about beneficial insects. I haven't always been fascinated by insects or even gardening, but I did spend a lot of time outside when I was young and I appreciate the dedication it takes to create a beautiful garden. Biology was my favorite topic in junior high and high school and I always looked forward to learning more about plants and animals. During my junior year in college, I had to make a tough decision about which class to take while earning my biology degree: entomology (insects) or lichenology (lichens). I opted for the entomology class because I didn't think collecting lichens sounded all that fun. My entomology professor was both interesting and funny, plus all the students got to make an insect collection as a lab project. Soon I had friends and family members from around the country sending me insects through the mail to help with my collection. My roommates were a little afraid to look in the freezer by the end of the semester! I learned about botany, microbiology, genetics, and soil science all in the same class and surprisingly it ended up being my favorite undergraduate course. I enjoyed incorporating different areas of science with entomology. I learned enough to know I just scratched the surface of entomology, and wanted to learn more.

So I ended up going to graduate school for a few years (many years if you ask my mom!) and became interested in research with insects. One major thread running through all my research was reducing the reliance of pesticides by using integrated pest management or IPM.

In many agricultural and horticultural systems, growers rely heavily on multiple insecticide applications to reduce insect feeding damage. Many of these products are broad spectrum, meaning they will kill a wide range of insects (good and bad) and have a long residual on plant tissue. Using broad spectrum insecticides in agriculture is warranted in some cases to preserve the quality of food for human consumption and reduce disease transmission. But in general, there are usually a few IPM tactics people can implement to reduce unnecessary insecticide usage. The utilization of IPM for homeowners is a perfect fit because many of the recommendations are practical and easy to learn, but I will go into that in the second chapter. I hope you enjoy this book about beneficial insects in the garden and learn why good bugs are an important part of creating a beautiful landscape.

ACKNOWLEDGMENTS

I was lucky enough to be surrounded by bright minds during my time in college. I would like to thank my peers and mentors because they inspired me to educate and promote the thriving science of entomology. I am grateful to Robert Koch, Ph.D. for many comments on improving this book.

No occupation is so delightful to me as the culture of the earth, and no culture comparable to that of the garden.

Thomas Jefferson

1

WHY ARE INSECTS IMPORTANT?

Maybe you are asking yourself if we really need insects in our lives. Insects are one of the most fascinating groups of animals alive today and should be celebrated whenever possible. Besides their beauty, insects are also diverse and abundant; surprisingly, there are more insects than any other plant or animal in the world. There are atbout one million insect species described so far, but some experts estimate there might be more than 10 million different kinds if we really looked. Each year, more than 3,500 insects are discovered throughout the world, particularly in tropical areas. Beetles are the most common kind of insect you are likely to see. In fact, one out of every five living animals is a beetle!

Insects are found in almost every type of environment, including rainforests, arid deserts, grasslands, forests, and agricultural or urban landscapes. Diversity and abundance have made insects successful animals throughout the world.

In addition to having sheer abundance, insects can also look spectacularly different. Variety has allowed insects to not only survive, but thrive in almost any niche. Insects can swim, live in soil, be attached to humans or reside on plants. Some adult insects can have horns or feather-like parts, while other insects can mimic leaves and twigs.

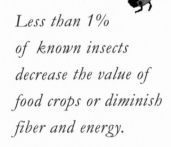

Less than 1% of known insects decrease the value of food crops or diminish fiber and energy.

The importance of insects in our lives cannot be fully appreciated until you know a little more about some of their negative and positive impacts. Very few insects are considered true pests, that is they transmit disease or destroy plants. Less than 1% of known insects decrease the value of food crops or diminish fiber and energy. There are a few insects that cause persistent problems throughout the world and are responsible for most of the negative consequences people associate with insects.

POLLINATION

A honey bee pollinating a flower

Insects provide many benefits and far outweigh the negative problems. Probably the most valuable economic gain we associate with insects is their pollination activity. Some plants, like almonds, alfalfa, and apples depend solely on insects to transfer pollen. These plants generate nectar and extra pollen that is attractive and nutritious to many different types of insects. While insects feed on these nourishing food sources, they transfer pollen around to other plants and trigger fertilization. Pollinating insects, like honey bees, produce other by-products humans find valuable. For example, bees wax makes a clean-burning candle, and royal jelly and bee pollen are used for dietary supplements. Other insect by-products include silk, shellac, dye, ink, and cosmetics.

DECOMPOSITION

In addition to pollination, insects also serve other beneficial roles in the environment and to our society. Some groups of insects, like dung beetles and blow flies, are decomposers that break down organic matter and release nutrients back into the soil. These decomposers accelerate the rate of decay and help create a layer of humus to cover the soil. Most decomposer insects follow a predictable pattern of breakdown on dead or decaying animal matter. As a result of their expected decomposition pattern, insects can help pinpoint the time of death for criminal forensic science cases.

FOOD CHAIN

Besides being efficient pollinators and decomposers, insects are part of the food chain. Small insects are eaten by large insects, and large insects are eaten by birds or other animals, and so on. Eventually the energy insects provide moves up the food chain until it reaches humans. In other cultures, humans eat insects because of their high protein content; some people even consider insects a delicacy! Although most insects are actually edible, examples of commonly eaten insects include bee and beetle larvae, grasshoppers, crickets, moth and butterfly caterpillars, and ants.

WHY CONSERVE AND ENCOURAGE NATURAL ENEMIES?

If your goal is to have a sustainable and productive garden, natural enemies are important assets. Natural enemies are considered beneficial because they eat other insects considered pests as part of their normal diet. Examples of common natural enemies include lady beetles, lacewings, and praying mantids. For most natural enemies, the immature stage (e.g., larvae or nymph) is the predatory life stage that actively seeks out prey. In other cases, the adult is the beneficial life stage and will consume insects along with nectar or pollen. Sometimes both the immature and adult life stages are beneficial and can eat hundreds of insects during their lifetime.

Promoting beneficial insects can reduce the negative impact of continuous pests. Because natural enemies eat other insects as part of their diet, they can help suppress the pest insects you don't want around. It is important to conserve the native, natural enemies you have and promote a diverse array of beneficial insects to stick around your yard. Fortunately, most common garden pests have at least one natural enemy. Soft-bodied insects, like aphids, are a common pest on

A lady beetle devours a pea aphid.

a number of different garden plants. Aphids are especially attractive to natural enemies because they are so numerous and easy to find on stems and leaves.

Natural enemies can help you reduce pesticide usage. When you depend on beneficial insects to reduce pests, you no longer have to rely on pesticides for control. Pesticides can be expensive, especially if you hire a professional applicator. The cost of pesticides quickly adds up if you have to make multiple applications in a year or over several years.

Reducing the reliance on pesticides has other advantages, including improving personal safety and minimizing unnecessary environmental hazards. There is always some level of risk associated with applying a pesticide. Many broad spectrum products are nerve toxins directed to kill a wide range of insects (hence the term broad spectrum). Insects and mammals have similar nervous systems, and therefore overexposure of some insecticides can make humans sick too. Often a broad spectrum application will kill beneficial and pollinating insects in addition to the target pest. Applying products above the recommended dosage is never recommended because of undue risk to humans and other animals.

The pedigree of honey does not
concern the bee, a clover, anytime,
to him, is aristocracy.

Emily Dickinson

2

IPM HISTORY AND CONCEPTS

An insect is considered to be a detrimental pest only by human opinion. Some insects can reduce yield in agricultural crops, vector disease, become a nuisance to animals, or cause aesthetic damage to ornamental plants. In those cases, humans wish those insects would just disappear! But the truth about insects is that they have been around a lot longer than humans (about 370 million years ago), and the notions of insects as "pests" was only fashioned with the beginning of organized agriculture (about 2500 BC).

INSECT CONTROL

Planning for insect control slowly progressed as agriculture and medicine became more advanced. Some of the earliest forms of control included breeding for resistant varieties and experimenting with chemicals. As the world's population dramatically increased in the 1800s, the switch from subsistence growing to commercial farming had a large impact on how people looked at insects. In general, people thought of insects as only harmful, causing significant loss to crops and causing disease.

As a result, insecticide use became more popular and a relatively quick fix for insect control in the early 1940s. Sometimes, very harsh chemicals were used to eliminate insects without regard to animal or environmental health. One of the most famous insecticides, DDT, was first used in 1941 and became very popular because it was cheap and killed many different kinds of insects. After World War II, insecticide development was a huge industry throughout the world and particularly in the United States.

During the 1950s, farmers wanted to completely eradicate common insect pests, and relied heavily on insecticides

Reducing reliance on insecticides by using proactive tactics to get rid of unwanted bugs is called Integrated Pest Management, or IPM.

for control. Fields would often be sprayed multiple times per year for several years in a row without monitoring for insects or other wildlife. Often beneficial insects and pollinators would needlessly be killed in addition to the target pest. In some crops, insects became genetically resistant to these commonly used chemicals and farmers were forced to approach pest problems differently. Genetically resistant insects have mutated genes that can withstand certain types of insecticides.

Ironically, the use of pest control without chemicals was also evolving at the same time as the big chemical boom. Scientists understood complete eradication was highly unlikely and that farmers had to establish a level of tolerance for insects. Instead of solely depending on chemical  control, farmers were encouraged to manage pests in a more holistic approach using several suppression tactics. Reducing the reliance of insecticides by incorporating several proactive tactics is called Integrated Pest Management, or IPM. Common IPM tactics include cultural, mechanical, physical, plant tolerance, and biological control to help reduce the reliance of chemical insecticides. Most gardeners can favorably reduce pest populations by modifying the plant environment with IPM. In general, insects are negatively impacted by any activity that disrupts its life cycle. But most gardeners keep plants maintained with high-energy inputs, like irrigation and fertilization, which ironically can promote rapid insect growth.

Altering existing growing conditions in the garden is an IPM tactic called cultural control. Often there are several management options gardeners can use to disrupt normal insect activity. Whenever thinking about cultural control of a common insect pest, always try to target the "weakest link" of the life cycle to maximize your efforts. For almost every insect, there is one stage that is particularly susceptible to environmental changes or food limitation. Two examples include the overwintering stage or the immature stage as the most negatively impacted by cultural control.

SANITATION

Sanitation is perhaps the most important and cost-effective cultural control method for gardeners. Remove weeds, volunteer plants, or dying vegetation to help eliminate any refuge for insects trying to breed, feed, or overwinter. Generalist pests, like spider mites and aphids, can survive on many different weedy plants. Leaf

Unwanted insects thrive in rotting fruit, which should be monitored and discarded.

litter, other debris, and wood piles can also harbor many different insects and sanitation will reduce the number of insects. Rotting and dropped fruit is considered ideal for insects to survive in and therefore should be continuously monitored and discarded.

IRRIGATION

Most garden plants need some kind of irrigation unless they are specifically adapted to low water use. Water management can also be used to control insects in several ways. Properly irrigated plants can tolerate more insect feeding, hence not showing stress as easily. Aphids and spider mites can thrive on a drought-stressed plant and feeding damage is often evident by yellowing or crinkling. The physical act of irrigation using a heavy stream of water will wash away many immature and soft-bodied insects. A few applications or water may be sufficient for pest management.

REDUCING LARGE MONOCULTURES AND MIXING UP PLANTING LOCATIONS

Other cultural control tactics include reducing large monocultures and mixing up planting locations of your commonly attacked plants. Monocultures, or a planting of a single type of plant, become very attractive to generalist and specialist insects. For example, if a garden only has roses in it (how boring!), the plant releases odors that become especially overwhelming to insects in the area and the roses will likely be infested over time. Instead, try to incorporate a variety of plant families to confuse insects looking for food and reproductive locations. Also alternate planting locations between years because continuously planting the same area in the garden makes for a predictable insect infestation. In other words, insects can more easily find a certain plant if it's always in the same location every year. This is especially important for insects that are not very mobile and have difficulty moving to new areas annually.

A garden full of only one kind of plant will release odors that will attract specific pests. The plant (roses, in this case) will likely become infested over time.

Have you ever wondered why you always get the same insects on the same plants at the same time of year? Because insects want to be successful and have become well-timed to emerge as their food does for optimal growth and reproduction. In some cases, people purposely plant their favorite nectar-producing plants at the same time because they want to attract butterflies and other beautiful insects to the garden every summer. Conversely, insects that cause significant damage will also try to synchronize with the garden. One way to disrupt insect success is to vary the planting dates of the most susceptible varieties. For example, planting vegetables before a persistent pest usually emerges will give young plants a few weeks of healthy pest-free growth. Another example is to stagger the planting dates so that plants are not all maturing at the same time.

MECHANICAL CONTROL

Mechanical control goes along with sanitation practices. Common examples of mechanical control include plant destruction. After

plants begin to decline, pruning back or removing dead tissue will make it difficult for insects to survive because they lose a food source. As most insects come in contact with the soil or soil surface at some point in the life cycle, mechanical control should not be overlooked as an IPM tactic. Tillage can also physically kill insects that are on plants and lingering in the soil. Consider careful pruning and destruction of woody plants that are infested with insects to prevent widespread damage of long-lived plants.

PHYSICAL CONTROL

Along with mechanical control, physical control can be a quick and easy method of reducing unwanted insects in the garden.

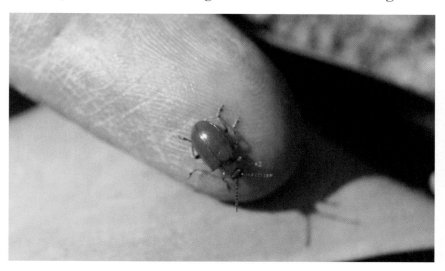

Physical control includes removing insects by hand.

Physical control simply means to remove insects from plants with your hands. If you are a bit squeamish about touching insects, some gardeners like to gently shake plants above a bucket of soapy water so that the insects fall inside. Eliminating large insects, like caterpillars, by hand can be an effective management IPM tactic because feeding immediately stops and subsequent generations are not produced.

INSECT TOLERANCE

Insect tolerance or resistance occurs in some plant cultivars, and should be used whenever persistent insect problems are noted. In tolerant plants, insect feeding will induce a response to help the plant recover; insects are not actually reduced, but plants are not as negatively affected by insect feeding as with susceptible plants.

> *Seek out tolerant plants for your garden. Pests are less productive and less likely to survive in an environment full of tolerant plants.*

Tolerant plants will look healthy longer and not show signs of stress, including wrinkling, discoloration, or wilting. Using tolerant plants is also important for garden aesthetics. Seek out tolerant plants when you are browsing through catalogs or looking in nursery greenhouses. Resistant plants are less commonly found, but are bred to reduce insect success; insects will not be as productive or survive as with susceptible plants. Resistant plants are especially useful if insects transmit a disease while feeding.

BIOLOGICAL CONTROL

Biological control is an IPM tactic that uses beneficial insects to control pest insects. Biological control in the garden often goes unnoticed unless you are specifically looking for it. In addition, broad spectrum insecticides can kill beneficial insects in the garden and prevent them from becoming established in your neighborhood. Sometimes biological control insects are not common in the garden because of inclement weather, such as a particularly harsh winter, or other difficult climatic changes. Beneficial insects have many obstacles to overcome before they can be successful. In general, natural enemies take longer to complete their life cycle, and usually produce fewer generations per year than common pests. For example, some lady beetles only complete one generation per year compared to some aphids that can complete fifteen generations in one year! Most predatory insects need to find a mate, sexually reproduce, and find suitable hosts, all of which can be very time consuming. In contrast, aphids asexually reproduce all summer and rarely have trouble finding suitable plants to start a colony.

CHEMICAL CONTROL

Chemical control is also a part of IPM, and has both advantages and disadvantages. Insecticides are very important in protecting our welfare, particularly in reducing insects that transmit disease. Chemical control has also improved farming practices by increasing soil conservation. Typically, insecticides are quick-acting and will stop insect feeding and reproduction within a day. Insecticides can be broad spectrum, killing a wide range of potential pests at the same time. Some broad spectrum products are also relatively cheap compared to using other IPM tactics. In spite of a few advantages, chemical control in the garden should be considered a last resort and only applied sparingly. As described in Chapter 1, chemical overuse on common insects will increase the likelihood of developing genetic resistance to insecticides. But overall,

insecticides can be highly toxic and pose an unnecessary health risk to humans and other animals.

There are effective "reduced risk" insecticides for reducing persistent pests in the garden. Reduced risk products can be more expensive and sometimes more difficult to find than traditional insecticides. But they offer many advantages for the environment, including reducing unnecessary toxin exposure to humans, birds, and other animals. Reduced risk products are relatively short-lived compared to broad spectrum products and should be considered for the garden whenever possible. For instance, horticultural soaps and oils are commonly used for aphids and other soft-bodied insects and only persist a few hours to several days. Reduced risk insecticides often target certain pests and leave behind pollinators and natural enemies. For example, a naturally occurring bacterium called *Bacillus thuringiensis*, or Bt, fatally disrupts the digestive system of an insect. These bacteria are very specific and can be purposely applied for insect control. There are several strains of Bt available for targeting different groups of insects (*kurstaki* for caterpillars, *israelensis* for flies and mosquitoes, and *tenebrionis* for beetles).

If you want to live and thrive,
let the spider run alive.

American Quaker Saying

3

HOW TO ENCOURAGE BENEFICIAL INSECTS IN YOUR GARDEN

Hopefully you have tried to look for insects in the garden and can recognize some as natural enemies that prey on and reduce common pests. But maybe you don't know where they came from or how to encourage more to visit your plants. In general, adult natural enemies seek out pollen and nectar to fuel migration, mating, and reproduction for the next generation. There are a few guidelines for making your garden look especially attractive to beneficial insects and maximizing their positive effects of pest management.

DIFFERENT NATIVE PLANTS

First, start with using as many different native plants as you can. Although exotic plants can often be big, beautiful, and flashy to our eyes, native natural enemies will not easily recognize them as a food source. So always try to incorporate native flowering plants in addition to the fancy varieties. Even though you may have a favorite plant you like to include and perhaps dominate the garden, consider planting a diverse mixture of plants whenever possible; assorted native flowers will likely attract different beneficial insects to the garden.

NECTAR AND POLLEN ACTIVITY

Second, plan for nectar and pollen availability all summer long. Seek out plants that have long-lived blooms so that adult natural enemies always have access to food. Short-lived plants can be included in the garden, but consider using flowers that bloom at different times of the year for continuous pollen production. Plants with easily accessible nectar and pollen are also favored by insects; small flowers may be more difficult for a wide or insects to feed. Remember not all plants have plentiful amounts of pollen and nectar for insects and other animals just because plants have obvious flowers.

Include in your garden plants with easily accessible nectar and pollen.

PURCHASING THE RIGHT INSECTS

Third, avoid purchasing adult insects for garden pest management. Without careful background research, there are several negative consequences to releasing imported insects in your garden. Most insects that can be purchased online or at gardening centers are not native to your area and are therefore not adapted to your unique growing conditions. Exotic insects intentionally released for pest management are not typically effective in a small-scale environment (like a personal garden) and will often fly away in search of a more suitable habitat. As a result of severe harvesting of insects for sale, these natural enemies are being depleted in their native habitat and are suffering detrimental consequences. Sometimes imported insects can become established and are more competitive than native ones; the exotic natural enemies could dominate the landscape and replace many of the native insects. An example of this is the multicolored Asian lady beetle reviewed in Chapter 5.

ATTRACTING INSECTS

Lastly, when creating a haven for natural enemies, mull over what might be attractive to insects looking for pollen and nectar. In most cases, insects have a preference for color, shape, and scent. Most insects cannot see red, but are strongly attracted to ultraviolet pigments that are not visible to humans. Incorporating a variety of flower colors in the garden will ensure attractiveness to many beneficial insects. Natural enemies might initially be attracted to an area because of the available pollen and nectar, but will not necessarily stay. In general, predatory insects like to generate offspring near a generous food supply of other insects. For example, lady beetles like to lay eggs on plants that

Incorporating a variety of flower colors in the garden will ensure attractiveness to many beneficial insects.

are infested with aphids because it ensures offspring will have food to eat when they hatch into larvae. Typically, immature insects are not very mobile and need food within a relatively short searching area.

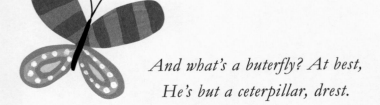

And what's a buterfly? At best,
He's but a ceterpillar, drest.

John Grey

4

COMMON PESTS IN THE GARDEN

Even though insects are present and actively feeding, it doesn't necessarily mean they have reached pest status. For example, one squash bug does not constitute an outbreak in the pumpkin patch. Every gardener has to establish a level of acceptance for insects on their plants. Ask yourself, "How many insects am I willing to tolerate?" Some people are very tolerant of insects in the garden and never want to use harsh chemicals for control. On the other end of the spectrum, there are some people who want a perfectly sterile and pristine garden and have no reservations about using chemicals as the primary means of control. But somewhere in the middle, most people try to incorporate a few IPM tactics and use chemicals in moderation. Before making drastic decisions about the insects in the garden, it is important to be able to recognize and differentiate between beneficial, harmful, or incidental insects. Realize that a garden can support literally thousands of insects without causing significant aesthetic damage to precious plants. Some people assume the garden is alive with pests and tend to neglect all the beneficial insects that might be out there too. Experts suggest less than 1% of all the insects are actually pests. With that small number in mind, learning to identify and monitor for insects that may become pests is vital to making effective management decisions. In addition to proper identification, understanding the time of year a particular insect can cause damage is essential. Again, anything you can do to disrupt the predictable activity of insects will greatly reduce their ability to thrive.

APHIDS

Some of the most common garden pests include the aphids. Aphids are small, soft-bodied insects that feed on plant sap with piercing sucking mouthparts. There are more than 1,300 different kinds of aphids in North America, and roughly 25% of all plants can be infested with aphids. Identifying different aphid species is difficult, but typically unnecessary for the home garden. The most common plant families to have aphids include the Compositae,

Colony of aphids

Rosaceae, and Coniferae. Heavily infested plants can look yellowed or wilted and be covered with numerous aphid cast molts. Adult aphids range from 1–10 mm long and have pear-shaped bodies. Although aphids can be almost any color, most are green, yellow, black, or brown. During the summer, aphids produce multiple generations by asexual cloning. Asexual reproduction shortens the life cycle and allows aphids to build up colonies very quickly. Typically aphids are wingless and are not highly mobile insects. However, when the food quality is poor or temperatures cool off, aphids will produce a winged generation that allows them to migrate to new plants. Aphids overwinter as eggs near the buds of woody plants. Often, aphids will not cause significant damage, but instead become a nuisance in the garden. Some aphids are capable of transmitting plant diseases, but this is more common in agricultural crops. Because aphids are liquid feeders, they excrete sugary honeydew that can make lawn furniture or cars sticky if under an infested plant. In most cases, aphids can be washed off plants with a strong stream of water and not require an insecticide treatment. Fortunately, many natural enemies like to eat aphids because they are often found in clustered colonies. In many cases, aphids are naturally controlled by native predatory insects. If aphids are persistently causing problems over multiple years, consider using dormant oil on woody plants at bud break or summer horticultural oil during the summer. Oils that come in contact with aphids or other insects act as a suffocant or smothering type of control agent.

SPIDER MITES

Another common nuisance pest in the garden is the spider mite. Spider mites are not actually insects, but arachnids more closely related to spiders and ticks. There are more than 200 different kinds of spider mites in North America, feeding on almost any type of plant, including fruits, vegetables, trees, and ornamentals. Heavily infested plants can look dirty or covered in a webbing, become yellowed or speckled and appear wilted. Severe infestations can weaken or kill plants. Spider mites are wingless and typically less than 1 mm in length, making them difficult to see with the naked eye. Body color is variable depending on the species, but ranges

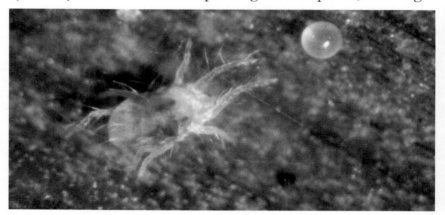

Two-spotted spider mite

from red, brown, green, and yellow. Spider mites can produce multiple generations per year and seem to do exceptionally well in hot, dry weather. Weeds and other volunteer plants provide refuge for spider mites when in transition between ornamental plants. Spider mites do have natural enemies, but often keeping plants properly irrigated will provide sufficient control. Like with aphids, a strong stream of water can wash off many of the mites, but several applications may be necessary for adequate control.

TRUE BUGS

There are more than 4,500 species of true bugs in North America. True bugs have piercing sucking mouthparts and most are herbivores that can damage flowers, seeds, and fruits in the garden. The most common true bugs throughout North America include boxelder bugs, squash bugs, stink bugs, and tarnished plant bugs. True bugs have piercing sucking mouthparts and are fluid feeders. Some true bugs are capable of transmitting, or vectoring, disease to plants. True bugs do not typically have as many natural enemies as aphids or spider mites, so other means of control should be considered for persistent problems. Sanitation is one of the most effective ways of reducing true bugs in the garden; removing weeds and dropped leaves will reduce potential eggs laying sites for

The wheel bug is one of the true bugs

females. Removing favorite plants will also discourage true bugs from your garden (e.g., female boxelder trees for boxelder bugs). Incorporating resistant plant varieties and minimizing dropped leaves can greatly reduce potential squash bug damage. Irrigating plant material or other structures where true bugs congregate will provide temporary relief. Horticultural soap can be effective at reducing immature true bugs, but is usually not capable of killing the adults. Soaps will break up the protective waxy coating of insects and will eventually cause them to completely dehydrate.

CATERPILLARS

Some of the most persistent garden pests are simply immature butterflies and moths. Ironically, most people like to see butterflies feeding on plant nectar and regard them as beautiful insects but

A swallowtail caterpillar

despise the immature stage for feeding on foliage. Caterpillars are defoliators and consume leaves, stems, and fruits. There are many different natural enemies of caterpillars, including parasitic wasps and flies, predatory true bugs, and lacewing larvae. Larger caterpillars can be removed by hand before they cause significant plant damage. Often butterflies and moths overwinter as eggs or resting pupae and simply breaking up the garden soil with tillage can provide effective control for the next season. Tillage will physically break apart the eggs and pupae or bring them closer to the soil surface. Another effective caterpillar control method is to use bacterium specifically targeted to insects. Products with *Bacillus thuringiensis*, or Bt, will damage the digestive tract of insects and cause them to stop feeding. Naturally occurring bacteria, like Bt, can be purchased and applied to the garden without reducing natural enemies.

THRIPS

With more than 600 different kinds of thrips in North America, it's no surprise they can invade gardens and become nuisance pests. Thrips are small and slender insects belonging in the order Thysanoptera. Thrips are less than 0.5 mm in length, but some can be more than 3 mm long. Body color is variable, but most

Thrips are very small, sometimes less than 0.5 mm in length.

are white or black; some adults have fringed wings while others are wingless. While there are predatory thrips common in the garden, many remove plant juices and are regarded as pests. Some thrips are capable of transmitting disease and are of economic concern. For example, the Western flower thrips, *Frankliniella occidentalis*, vectors tomato spotted wilt virus. Although healthy

plants can usually tolerate thrips feeding, heavily infested plants will look stunted, wilted, or contorted. Thrips prefer to feed in flower clusters or other enclosed parts of a plant, and as a result, are often overlooked as causing plant damage. Sometimes thrips will cause a stippling on the flower petals that is blamed on spider mites. Because most thrips are quite small, the best way to look for infestations is to gently shake a flower over a white piece of paper. Dark or translucent thrips will drop out of the flower and begin to run around the paper. Minimizing the negative effects from thrips feedings starts with removing weeds or volunteer plants around the garden to reduce potential food sources. There are also many resistant varieties available for thrips and should be incorporated for persistent thrips problems. Pruning heavily infested limbs and flowers or using reflective mulch can also be highly effective for thrips control.

Ladybug! Ladybug!
Fly away home.
Your house is on fire.
And your children are all gone.

Children's Nursery Rhyme

5

LADY BEETLES

S ome of the most important beneficial insects in the garden are lady beetles, sometimes called ladybugs or ladybird beetles. Lady beetles are in the order Coleoptera and family Coccinellidae. There are nearly 450 different species of lady beetles in North America, and they can be quite variable in size, shape, and coloration. As with all beetles, lady beetles have chewing mouthparts as larvae and adults. Therefore, lady beetles become especially important because most adults and larvae are predatory against garden pests. So instead of just one stage being beneficial, two stages eat other insects as part of their everyday diet.

HABITATS, CHARACTERISTICS, AND BEHAVIOR

Most lady beetles take a year to complete a generation, but some beetles can have multiple generations per year. During the summer, lady beetles can be found in many different habitats, including agricultural, urban, forest, and other places where soft-bodied insects, like aphids, are found. The adults are the most common overwintering stage, finding sheltered areas for protection against the cold. During the winter, you can commonly find lady beetles

Lady beetles are among the most important beneficial insects.

under logs, leaves, and bark. Sometimes beneficial lady beetles become a nuisance to homeowners in the winter because adults are attracted to heat and shelter inside the home. If they become a problem, simply vacuum up the adults around windowsills to prevent them from moving throughout the house.

In general, adults are rounded and between 3–8 mm in length. They are protected by armor-like front wings called elytra. The front wings meet in a straight line and do not overlap like some other insects (e.g., squash bugs). The elytra are often compared to a turtle shell and are brightly colored orange, red, and black. The bright coloration might help deter larger predators, such as birds, from attack. Adults don't use the front wings to fly, but depend on the hind wings for flight. For some lady beetles, their heads are tucked under a protective shield called a pronotum. Lady beetles have club-like antennae that can aid in finding suitable food and mates. Adult lady beetles have walking legs but can move around a plant quickly if needed. As temperatures warm up in the spring, adults will move to plants and actively look for places to mate and feed. In addition to devouring insects, adult lady beetles will eat pollen, nectar, and honeydew to get additional energy to survive and produce the next generation.

After mating, females will look for a place to lay eggs. She is

looking for a place that will offer food to the newly hatched larvae; so plants infested with aphids or other insects are considered prime locations! Females will lay football-shaped eggs in small clusters, ranging from 5–20 eggs. Depending on the lady beetles species, a female is capable of laying a few hundred eggs in during the summer. Eggs first appear white or creamy in color, but can turn yellow, orange, or gold as they mature. Eggs will hatch in

Lady beetle larvae eating an aphid

about 7 days, depending on the temperature. If the weather is exceptionally warm, eggs could hatch in 4–5 days.

When the lady beetle eggs hatch, small larvae emerge and begin to look for food immediately. Lady beetle larvae are especially mobile and will aggressively hunt down prey. Usually larvae are dark grey or black with white, orange, red or yellow markings, and are covered with spines. Because lady beetle larvae can look menacing, they can be mistaken for pests in the garden. But larvae are like hungry teenagers and can consume many soft-bodied insects over a short period of time. Over the next 10–21 days, larvae will continue to eat and increase in size with several molting periods. As lady beetle larvae reach their maximum size (nearly that of the adults), they look for a place to pupate.

The pupal case looks very different than the larval or adult stages, and can be mistaken for other insects or plant disease. The pupal stage is when the lady beetles are developing wings and reproductive organs. Often pupae are attached to a plant surface. It's important to leave the pupal cases on the plants so that they can complete development. It may take 7 days before the adults emerge from the pupal case. The entire life cycle of lady beetles can range from 4–7 weeks, depending on the species and temperature.

IN THE GARDEN

Although there are likely to be several different kinds of lady beetles in the garden, there are a few species that are more common in  areas with native flowering plants. Some of the most common species include the convergent lady beetle, multicolored Asian lady beetle, pink-spotted lady beetle, seven-spotted lady beetle, two-spotted lady beetle, and twice-stabbed lady beetle. As you probably noticed, most of the common names arise from what the front wing covers look like—how clever!

CONVERGENT LADY BEETLE

The convergent lady beetle, *Hippodamia convergens*, is a common predator throughout North America. Adults are 6–7 mm long and oval shaped. The elytra are orange or red and have 13 black spots. The pronotum is black with two converging white lines.

Convergent lady beetles

Both larvae and adults like to eat aphids and other soft-bodied insects. The convergent lady beetle is capable of producing several generations a year if food is available and the weather is cooperative.

MULTICOLORED ASIAN LADY BEETLE

The multicolored Asian lady beetle, *Harmonia axyridis*, is a relatively new predator in North America. But since the early 1980s, this predator has spread throughout the United States and Canada. This species is particularly aggressive and sometimes will dominate over native lady beetles. As the common name

Multicolored Asian lady beetles

suggests, the multicolored Asian lady beetle can appear in various colors and spotting patterns. The elytra range from yellow to red to black with 0–20 spots possible. Adults are about 5–8 mm long and considerably round or dome shaped; the pronotum often appears to have an "M" on it. Both the larvae and adults prefer to feed on aphids as their main food source. The multicolored Asian lady beetle is considered a pest in some areas because of their tendency to enter homes to overwinter.

PINK-SPOTTED LADY BEETLE

Pink-spotted lady beetle

The pink-spotted lady beetle, *Coleomegilla maculata*, is a native predator to North America. Adults are 5–6 mm long and the elytra are pink in color. The elytra have ten black spots, with additional two black spots on the pronotum. Pink-spotted lady beetle larvae are black with orange markings on the back. Although the larvae and adults are excellent predators of aphids, the adults may rely on plant pollen more than other lady beetles.

SEVEN-SPOTTED LADY BEETLE

Seven-spotted lady beetle

The seven-spotted lady beetle, *Coccinella septempunctata*, is another relatively new beneficial insect in North America. This species was introduced in the 1970s because it was considered beneficial against aphids. Compared to other lady beetles they are relatively large and range from 7–8 mm. The body is oval or dome shaped with bright red elytra. There are 7 black spots on the elytra, but also take note of the white spots on the side of the head. Both the larvae and adults eat aphids, scales, and other immature insects.

TWICE-STABBED LADY BEETLE

Twice-stabbed lady beetle

The twice-stabbed lady beetle, *Chilocorus stigma*, can be found throughout North America (except they don't occur west of the Sierra Nevada region). Adults are 3–5 mm long, dome shaped, and are shiny black with two large red spots on the elytra. The twice-stabbed lady beetle has two generations per year in most parts of North America, but can have more in the southern United States. Larvae and adults prefer to live in trees and hunt for armored scales, aphids, and other immature insects.

How doth the little busy bee
Improve each shining hour,
And gather honey all the day
From every opening flower!

Isaac Watts

6

OTHER BEETLES

In addition to the lady beetles, there are several other kinds of beetles that are effective natural enemies, including ground beetles, rove beetles, and tiger beetles. Beetles are in the order Coleoptera and make up the largest group of insects. With more than 30,000 different beetles found in North America, it is no surprise that there is an abundance of predatory beetles in the garden.

The ground beetles are a large group of predatory insects in the family Carabidae. The adults and larval stages are considered beneficial and will eat almost any type of insect. There are more than 3,000 different kinds of ground beetles in North America and they range from 6–30 mm in length. Many will have a solid, shiny black body; some ground beetles have a black body and iridescent red, purple, or green markings on the forewings.

Most ground beetles have a relatively long body, flattened head, threadlike antennae, and long legs. As the name suggests, adults prefer to run on the ground and rarely fly. In general, adults are actively hunting on the ground at night and hide under rocks or debris during the day.

COMMON BLACK GROUND BEETLE

Common black ground beetle

Another familiar type of ground beetle in the northern United States and Canada is the common black ground beetle, *Pterostichus melanarius*. There are more than 200 different *Pterostichus* species with the same common name because they look similar. Adults range from 12–20 mm in length and have shiny black forewings with obvious grooves and enlarged mandibles for grasping prey. Common black ground beetle adults are commonly seen in from July through September in gardens, fields, and moist woods. Adults are nocturnal feeders that eat a variety of insects, including other beetles. During the day, adults can be found under rocks, wood chips, or other debris. Common black ground beetles have one generation per year, but some adults can survive two or more years.

FIERY SEARCHER

One common type of ground beetle native to North America and found throughout the United States and Canada is the fiery searcher, *Calosoma scrutator*. Fiery searchers are also known as caterpillar hunters because they like to feed on all types of caterpillars. Adults range from 25–35 mm in length and are a beautiful shiny green with red and gold borders on the forewings. Fiery hunters are commonly seen in the spring, but are actively

Fiery searcher

feeding all spring, summer, and fall. Sometimes adults are visible in trees, but are most often hunting in gardens, fields, and wooded areas. Fiery hunters have one generation per year, but adults can live up to three years.

ROVE BEETLE

In addition to the ground and tiger beetles, the rove beetles are

Rove beetle

another large group of predatory insects. Rove beetles are in the family Staphylinidae and more than 3,000 different species are found in North America. Rove beetles are predators of other insects but will also eat decaying vegetative matter. The adults are very easily distinguished from other beetles because they have shortened forewings that expose the end of the abdomen. Although rove beetles can fly, the adults are more often seen running on the ground. Adults are shiny brown or black, have enlarged mandibles for grasping prey, and range in size from 2–20 mm in length. Most rove beetle species are predatory, including the adult and larval stages. Rove beetles can be found under rocks or wood or around mushrooms or other decaying vegetation. Some rove beetle display a defensive behavior—similar to scorpions when disturbed—of raising the abdomen.

TIGER BEETLES

Tiger beetle

One of the most fantastic groups of beetles is the tiger beetles in the family Cicindelidae. There are more than 200 different species of tiger beetles in North America and are closely related to the ground beetles. Adults and larvae are predatory and will consume almost any type of insect. Tiger beetle adults are often brightly colored and metallic blue, green, or orange. But some are more camouflaged in their environment. They range from 10–20 mm in length. Adults have long legs and are quick runners. Tiger beetles are considered ambush feeders and will seize prey with powerful sickle-like mandibles. The S-shaped larvae construct vertical burrows in dry soil and wait for prey to fall inside. Tiger beetles have one generation per year and commonly hunt during the day in gardens, stream edges, forests, and deserts.

With six small diamonds for his eyes
He walks upon the summer skies,
Drawing from his silken blouse
The lacework of his dwelling house.

Robert P. Tristram Coffin

7

ANTLIONS AND LACEWINGS

A ntlions and lacewings are often overlooked as beneficial insects in the garden. Sometimes the larvae are even mistaken for harmful or destructive insects. Antlions and lacewings are grouped together in the order Neuroptera because they have mesh-like wings made up of many veins. Both pairs of wings are oval in shape and similar in size and are held straight and roof-like over the back at rest. Both antlions and lacewings are soft-bodied insects with long antennae. There are about 330 different kinds of neuropteran insects in North America.

ANTLIONS

Antlions resemble damselflies in many ways, but have longer, clubbed antennae. Antlions can reach up to 45 mm and have

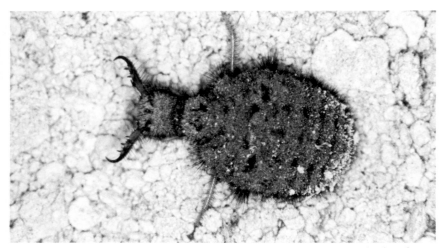

Antlion larvae

a wingspan of 65 mm. Like the lacewings, antlions are poor flyers and have transparent wings with many veins. Instead of laying eggs on stalks like the lacewings, mated female antlions will deposit eggs into the sand. Eggs will hatch into aggressive predatory larvae called "doodlebugs." As the name suggests, antlions like to eat ants, but will also prey on other small insects. Some doodlebugs will hide among debris to capture prey, while others make sand pit traps and wait for unsuspecting prey to fall down the sloping sides.

Antlion

Doodlebugs can continue to eat for two years and molt three times before they begin pupation. Antlions will pupate in a silken cocoon and remain within the sandy soil for about one month. Adult antlions will emerge from the soil and are brown in color. In general, they live for about one month and feed on other insects, pollen, and nectar. Adults are active at night and are rarely seen during the day because they are camouflaged in with plants. The most common antlion throughout North America is Myrmeleon formicarius.

LACEWINGS

Lacewings go through at least two generations per year. The entire life cycle takes about 4 weeks, but is highly dependant on temperature. Mated female lacewings will lay eggs on almost any plant foliage infested with soft-bodied insects like aphids. Individual eggs are attached to a hair-like filament or stalk. The egg stalk is about 9 mm long and helps protect the egg from predation by other insects. After a few days, the eggs will hatch into small alligator-like larvae.

The larvae are the predatory stage and are considered voracious eaters. Lacewing larvae are brownish and have large, sickle-shaped jaws for grasping and killing prey.

Although lacewing larvae will feed on spider mites, whiteflies, and thrips, they prefer to feed on aphids and are sometimes known as "aphid lions." After 2–3 weeks of feeding and molting three times, larvae will eventually reach about 9.5 mm long and begin to pupate. When lacewing larvae pupate, they spin a silken cocoon that resembles a miniature cotton ball. During the pupal stage, lacewings are developing their wings and reproductive organs. It's important not to dislodge the pupal case from the undersides of plants because they will not likely survive to the adult stage. After about 5 days, adult lacewings will emerge from the pupal cases and will begin mating.

Adult lacewings also have chewing mouthparts, and will eat pollen, nectar, and other insects. Adults are about 18–19 mm long and have threadlike antennae at least as long as the body. Adults can survive for about 5–6 weeks. Lacewings aren't considered great flyers and will often flutter around to different plants. Adults are usually in the overwintering stage but will not survive extremely cold weather conditions. Adults will seek out leaf litter or other protective areas to survive the winter. There are a couple common lacewings you are likely to see in the garden, including green and brown species.

BROWN LACEWINGS

Brown lacewing

Brown lacewings are more commonly encountered in wooded areas and are considered excellent predators. In general, brown lacewings are tan in color and smaller than green lacewings. Both the adult and larval stages are predatory. In most areas, brown lacewings become active earlier in the season compared to green lacewings and may help contribute to early-season pest control. Some brown lacewing larvae cover themselves in debris for protection and are

called "trashbugs." The most common species of brown lacewing, *Hemerobius stigma*, ranges from 5–7.5 mm long.

GREEN LACEWINGS

There are two common green lacewings you are likely to see on aphid-infested plants. *Chrysoperla carnea* is the most common green lacewing throughout North America, while *Chrysoperla rufilabris*

is more common in southeastern and Midwestern United States. Green lacewings adults range from 12–20 mm long and only feed on pollen, nectar, and honeydew. Adults have pale green bodies, golden eyes, and transparent wings.

Green lacewing

Two-legged creatures we are supposed to love as we love ourselves. The four-legged, also, can come to seem pretty important. But six legs are too many from the human standpoint.

Joseph W. Krutch

8

PARASITOID WASPS
AND PARASITIC FLIES

Parastic flies and parasitoid wasps are another important group of natural enemies in the garden. Adult parasitic flies and parasitoid wasps eat nectar and deposit eggs on or in other insects or animals. These beneficial insects naturally attack a wide range of insects, including aphids, caterpillars, and true bugs, and can help control insect outbreaks in the garden. There are distinct differences between predators, parasitoids, and parasites. Usually predators consume many prey items during a lifetime; for example, lady beetles can eat hundreds of aphids during the larval and adult stages. Parasitoids will only use and kill one prey item during a lifetime. Eventually the host will die as the parasitoid wasp larva grows inside the body cavity and the new adult will emerge. Parasites usually attack a host in great numbers but do not kill the host. Examples of the parasitic insects include fleas and lice. When the parasitic eggs hatch, they begin to consume the host as a food source. Sometimes multiple eggs are laid on a single host, such as with caterpillars.

PARASITIC FLIES

Parasitic flies are also common to see in the garden, even though most people see the adults as nuisance insects. Parasitic flies are in the order Diptera and are closely related to house flies, mosquitoes, and midges. As with the parasitic wasps, identifying parasitic flies is difficult because they are so numerous. The most commonly seen parasitic flies include tachinids, bee flies, and hover flies. There are also a number of other parasitic flies not mentioned here. Immature flies are called maggots and can be described as white and legless larvae.

BEE FLIES

The bee flies belong to the family Bombyliidae and have more than 750 species in North America. Adult bee flies closely mimic bees in coloration and flying behavior, but are harmless because they do not have a sting. The adults are stout, hairy, may have strong yellow and black banding patterns, and range from 7–15 mm in

Bee fly

length. Larvae feed on caterpillars, beetle larvae, wasps and bees, and other insects.

TACHINID FLIES

The tachinid flies belong in the large family Tachinidae and have more than 1,300 different species in North America. Adult

Tachinid fly

tachinids resemble stocky house flies with black or grey bodies and range from 3–14 mm in length. Females prefer to lay eggs on caterpillars or beetle larvae.

PARASITOID WASPS

Parasitoid wasps belong in the order Hymenoptera and are related to bees, ants, and other wasps, such as yellowjackets; however most parasitoid wasps are stingless. Parasitic wasps can be distinguished from stinging wasps because they have long antennae and are generally much smaller in size (1–15 mm long). Parasitoid wasps will often attack aphids and other soft-bodied insects. As the egg hatches and begins to feed inside the body cavity, the aphid becomes enlarged and puffy. Infected aphids are sometimes called "mummies" and are indications of beneficial parasitoid wasp activity.

> *Most parasitoid wasps are stingless. They can be distinguished by their long antennae and small size.*

Because of their small size, identifying parasitoid wasps is very difficult even for trained entomologists. Parasitoid wasps generally fall into one of two superfamilies, Chalcidoidea and Ichneumonoidea. Experts believe there are more than 60,000 species in Chalcidoidea and more than 80,000 species in Ichneumonoidea throughout the world. A common family of parasitic wasps found throughout North America is called the Ichneumonids. Adults range from 3–75 mm in length and have an elongated abdomen. Females are black, slender, and have a long ovipositor.

The Ichneumon wasp is a common parasitic wasp in North America.

Aleiodes indiscretus wasp parasitizing a gypsy moth caterpillar.

The spider's touch,
how exquisitely fine!
Feels at each thread,
and lives along the line.

Alexander Pope

9

OTHER PREDATORY INSECTS AND CLOSE RELATIVES

Chapters 5–8 covered some of the most common beneficial insects seen in the garden. However, there are many other kinds of insects and insect-relatives that can reduce harmful insects naturally. For example, there are praying mantids and predatory true bugs found throughout most of North America. Although not insects, spiders and predatory mites are common in almost every garden and provide excellent insect control.

PRAYING MANTIDS

There are only eleven different kinds of praying mantids in North America, all belonging to the order Mantodea. Mantids are most closely related to grasshoppers and cockroaches, but are easily distinguished from other insects. Mantids have a large head

Praying mantids provide excellent insect control.

with obvious eyes and powerful chewing mouthparts. Mantids can literally look over their shoulders because they have a very flexible neck. Praying mantids are predatory as nymphs or adults and have specialized legs for grasping prey. The first pair of legs is modified for striking, and almost any insect is an acceptable food source. Mantids are also cannibalistic if other insects are difficult to find. Females will deposit protective egg cases called oothecae. Often the egg cases will be sold commercially to enhance biological control in the garden.

Praying mantids are predatory as both nymphs and adults.

One of the most common mantids found throughout the eastern United States and Canada is the European mantid, *Mantis religiosa*. Adults can be brown or green in color with a black spot on the first pair of legs, and range from 50–65mm in length. The European mantid actively feeds during the day, and prefers areas with mixed vegetation. Another common mantid is called the Chinese mantid, *Tenodera aridifolia*. Adults can be pale green or tan and range from 65–85 mm in length. Chinese mantids prefer meadow and gardens to seek out various types of prey, including caterpillars, bees, and moths.

COMMON PREDATORY BUGS

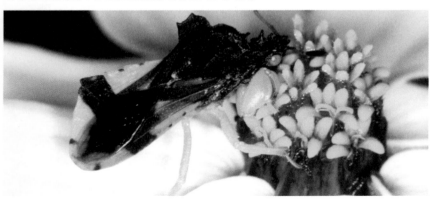

Ambush bugs are among the common predatory bugs.

Although some true bugs are considered pests in the garden, there are a many predatory species common in gardens. All true bugs belong in the order Hemiptera and have piercing-sucking mouthparts that remove fluids from plants or other animals. True bugs have wings that cross over the back at rest, but sometimes the wings can be reduced. Sometimes the first pair of legs is modified for grasping prey, as with the praying mantids. Common predatory bugs include: ambush bugs, assassin bugs, big-eyed bugs, damsel bugs, minute pirate bugs, and stink bugs.

Damsel bug, another common predatory bug

STINK BUGS

One of the most common predatory stink bugs found throughout North America is called the spined soldier bug, *Podisus maculiventris*. Stink bugs belong in the family Pentatomidae. The spined solider bug is light brown or tan and can be speckled with black spots. Adults range from 10–12 mm in length and

Stink bug

have obvious spines on each side of the body. These stink bugs prefer to be in areas with mixed vegetation, including crops and gardens where they prey on caterpillars and beetle larvae. A common big-eyed bug is the large *Geocoris bullatus*. As the name suggest, big-eyed bugs have large, bulging eyes and a broad head. Adults are oval, grey, and about 3 mm long. Big-eyed bugs feed on almost anything smaller than themselves.

ARACHNIDS

Spider webs can be a menacing sight for some, but most spiders are not particularly aggressive unless threatened.

Garden spider in its web

Besides the insects, there are many diff-erent arachnids common to gardens. Arachnids and insects are closely related and share many of the same characteristics. Spiders are arachnids and can provide excellent effective biological control against insect pests. There are more than 3,000 different kinds of spiders in North America, with quite a variety of color patterns and body size. Spiders can be found in almost every habitat insects can be found. All spiders are predatory and use venom to subdue prey for themselves or their offspring. Some spiders spin a sticky web to trap and store insects. Many people do not like to see spiders or spider webs around the home and will try to remove them. But in most cases, spiders are not particularly aggressive unless threatened and generally their venom is harmless to humans.

GLOSSARY

abdomen. The third major body region of an insect, following the head and thorax, where digestion, excretion, and respiration occur.

antennae. Pair of segmented appendages located on the head near the eyes used for sensory.

appendages. Any part attached by a segmented joint to the body, including legs and antennae.

aquatic. Adapted to life in water; living in water.

arboreal. Living in, on, or among trees.

biological control. The use of living organisms to control or suppress undesirable animals and plants.

carnivorous. A flesh eater; see herbivorous and phytophagous.

caterpillar. Larva of butterflies, moths, or skippers (Lepidoptera).

chewing mouthparts. Mouthparts with mandibles fitted for chewing.

diurnal. Active or flying during the day; see nocturnal.

elytra. The leathery, hardened forewing of beetles (Coleoptera) and earwigs (Dermaptera) forming a cover to protect the hindwings and abdomen; see hemelytra and tegmina.

exoskeleton. The external skeleton made up of a hardened cuticle and where the muscles are attached.

forensic entomology. Any legal activity involving insects.

forewings. The first pair of wings attached to the thorax; can be thickened to protect the hindwings and abdomen.

frass. Insect excrement often mixed with plant or animal fragments.

grub. A generalized term used to describe a larva, particularly a scarab beetle (Coleoptera: Scarabeidae).

head. First major body region, before the thorax and abdomen, where the brain, mouthparts, eyes, and antennae are located.

hemelytra. Basal portion or anterior forewing which is thickened in certain Hemiptera; see elytra and tegmina.

herbivorous. Feeding on non-woody plant tissue; see carnivorous and phytophagous.

hibernation. A period of temporary dormancy, usually during the winter, to avoid certain harsh environmental conditions.

hindwings. The second pair of wings attached to the thorax.

honeydew. Sugary fluid excreted from fluid-feeders such as aphids and leafhoppers (Hemiptera).

host. The organism in which a parasite or parasitoid lives on or in during its development.

immature. The life stage before the adult commonly referred to as nymph or larva.

instar. Stage between molts of immature insects.

larva. The immature stage between the egg and pupal stages of insects with complete metamorphosis. Note: the term larva is now often incorrectly used to describe the immature stages of all insects, including those with simple or incomplete metamorphosis; see nymph.

leg. One of three paired jointed appendages of the thorax; used for locomotion, defense and bringing food to the mouth.

life cycle. The series of developmental changes insects undergo to sustain a population, including fertilization, reproduction and death.

macrodecomposers. Organisms that break down large pieces of organic matter into small pieces.

maggot. Legless larva lacking a distinct head usually used to describe certain flies (Diptera).

mating. The sequence of events surrounding the insemination of the female by the male.

membranous wings. Thin and transparent wings, examples include dragonflies (Odonata) and lacewings (Neuroptera).

metamorphosis. Series of changes an insect passes through in its growth from egg to adult.

migration. Mass movement, typically by flight.

molting. Shedding of the exoskeleton and development of a new cuticle to increase overall body size and sometimes to attain more adult features.

monophagous. Feeding on only one kind of food, such as one plant species; see omnivorous and polyphagous.

nectar. Sugary secretion of the plant, produced by the flowers; a food source for many insects, including beetles, butterflies, moths, and flies.

niche. Specialized geographical location or unique habitat for feeding or breeding.

nocturnal. Active or flying at night; see diurnal.

nymph. An immature stage of insects with simple metamorphosis; see larva.

omnivorous. Feeding generally on animal or vegetable food or both.

organism. An organic entity.

oviposit. To deposit or lay eggs.

parthenogenesis. Egg development without fertilization; an example is aphids (Hemiptera).

parasite. Any organism that lives in or on another host to obtain shelter or food; typically does not kill the host; see host, hyperparasitism and parasitoid.

parasitoid. Any organism that lives in or on another host to obtain shelter and food; typically will kill the host; see host and parasite.

pest. Any unwanted and destructive animal that attacks plants or animals.

piercing-sucking mouthparts. Mandibles and maxillae have been modified for piercing plant or animal tissue; examples include aphids (Hemiptera) and mosquitoes (Diptera).

polyphagous. Eating many different kinds of food; see monophagous and omnivorous.

predaceous. Living by preying upon other organisms as larve or adults; examples are beetles, dragonflies and praying mantids.

predator. An organism that kills other animals for food as an energy source.

proboscis. Any extended mouth structure; examples include aphids, true bugs, butterflies, moths and mosquitoes.

pupa. The inactive stage, between larva and adult, of insects that go through complete metamorphosis; called chrysalids in butterflies (Lepidoptera), cocoons in moths (Lepidoptera) and puparia of certain flies (Diptera) (plural, pupae).

pupate. To become a pupa.

rasping-sponging mouthparts. Slashing mouthparts that cut animal skin followed by sponging mouthparts that soak up blood.

scavenger. An animal that feeds on dead plants, animals, decaying materials or animal wastes.

sponging mouthparts. An advanced fly (Diptera) with non-biting mouthparts lacking stylets in which liquid is sopped up.

tegmina. A hardened, leathery forewing with reduced wing venation typically found in grasshoppers (Orthoptera); see elytra and hemelytra.

thorax. The second major body region, between the head and abdomen, of the insect body where the legs and wings are attached.

Definitions were adapted, in part, by the Torre-Bueno Glossary of Entomology (Stephen W. Nichols, New York: New York Entomological Society, 1989).

PHOTO CREDITS

Below are the list of credits for each photograph in order according to the page number on which it is found. All pages with photographs not listed below are found on the following websites: www.photos.com and www.123rf.com.

Photographs courtesy of Jon Sullivan, pdphoto.org, on pages 15 and 54

Photographs by Jim Kalisch, University of Nebraska Department of Entomology on pages 45, 47, 50, 60, 61, 66, 68, 74, 79, 86, 92, 93

Photographs courtesy of Jeff Delonge, ©Entomart, http://www.entomart. be/contact.html, on pages 69 (http://www.entomart.be/listetotale.html) and 78 (http://home.tiscali.be/entomart.ins/Mylabrisquadri.html)

Photograph courtesy of Bruce Marlin - www.cirrusimage.com on page 83

Photograph courtesy of Rayanne Lehman, Pennsylvania Department of Agriculture, Bugwood.org on page 63

Photograph courtesy of Stephen Ausmus, ARS Photo Library http://www. ars.usda.gov/is/graphics/photos/feb04/k11013-1.htm on page 32

Photograph courtesy of Scott Bauer, ARS Photo Library http://www.ars. usda.gov/is/graphics/photos/on pages 18 and 87

REFERENCES

This book is not intended to be a field guide for insect identification, but instead describes groups of insects that provide biological control in the garden. There are excellent references available for those wanting to learn more about specific identification and distribution information.

1. *Field Guide to North American Insects and Spiders*, National Audubon Society. ISBN 0394507630.
2. *Garden Insects of North America*, Whitney Cranshaw. ISBN 0691095604.
3. *Handbook of Vegetable Pests*, John Capinera. ISBN 0121588610.

INDEX

Created with TExtract © Texyz 2008

AUTHOR

Erin W. Hodgson is an assistant professor in the Department of Biology at Utah State University and serves as an entomologist for the university's extension program. Erin is a member of the Utah Plant Pest Diagnostic Laboratory. She received her Ph.D. in entomology in 2005 and has a background in integrated pest management for agriculture and horticulture. Through the university's extension program, Erin educates the public about beneficial and harmful insects. She regularly participates in the Utah State University Extension Master Gardener Program and creates educational outreach materials for homeowners.